Tana Hoban

Greenwillow Books
New York

Library of Congress
Cataloging in Publication Data
Hoban, Tana.
Take another look.
Summary: By viewing nine
subjects both in full-page photos
and through die-cut pages, the
reader learns that things may
be perceived in different ways.
1. Perception—Juvenile literature.
2. Selectivity (Psychology)
—Juvenile literature.
[1. Visual perception]
I. Title.   BF311.H565
152.1′4   80-21342
ISBN 0-688-80298-2
ISBN 0-688-84298-4 (lib. bdg.)

This one is
for Ada

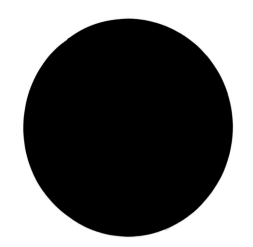

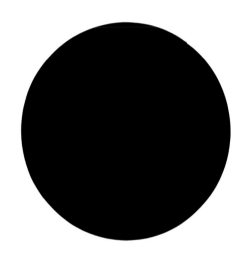

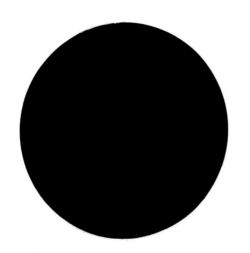

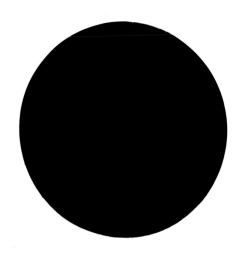

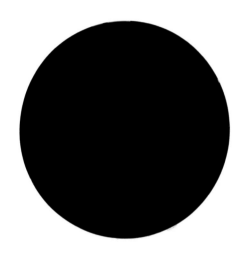

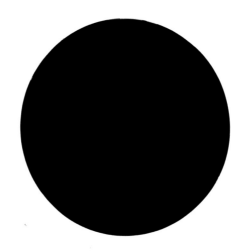

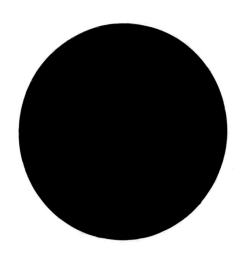

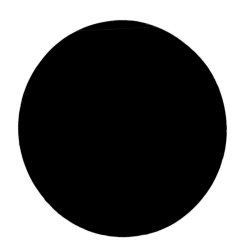

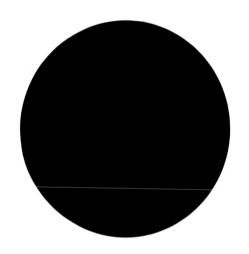

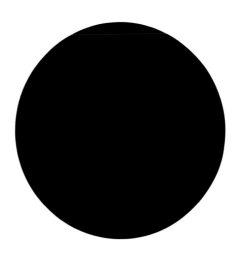

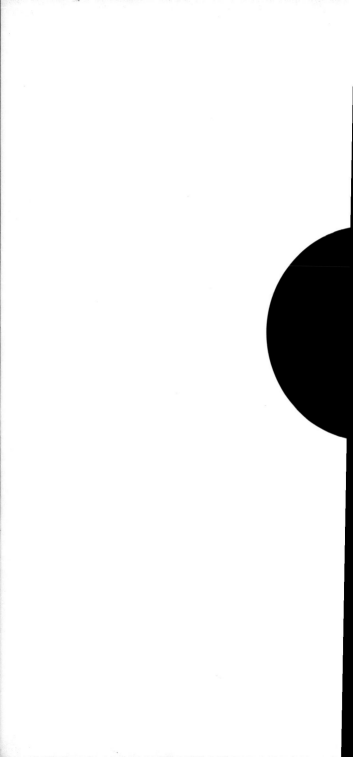

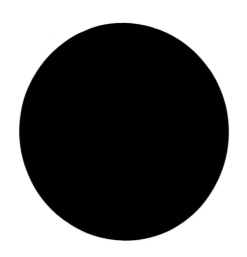

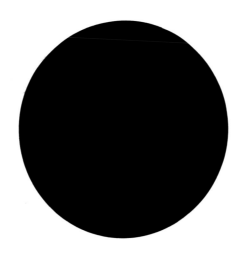

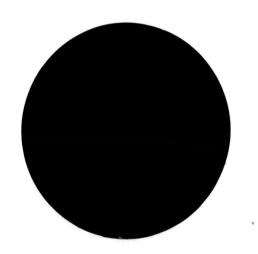

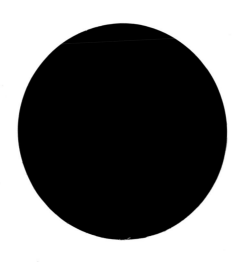

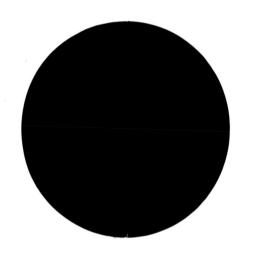

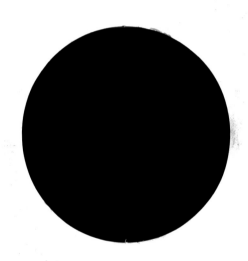